DINOSAURS
Preschool Basics Workbook

This book belongs to:

_____

_____

Copyright © 2019 by KIDSFUN

All rights reserved. No part of this publication may be reproduced, distributed, or transmitted in any form or by any means, including photocopying, recording, or other electronic or mechanical methods, without the prior written permission of the publisher, except in the case of brief quotations embodied in critical reviews and certain other non-commercial uses permitted by copyright law.

Table of Contents

Number Tracing.

Let's Count!

Match the Number.

What a Difference.

More or Less?

Big vs. Small.

Compare sizes.

The picture that comes next!

Number Fun.

0 Zero

Trace the number 0. Color the **Zero**

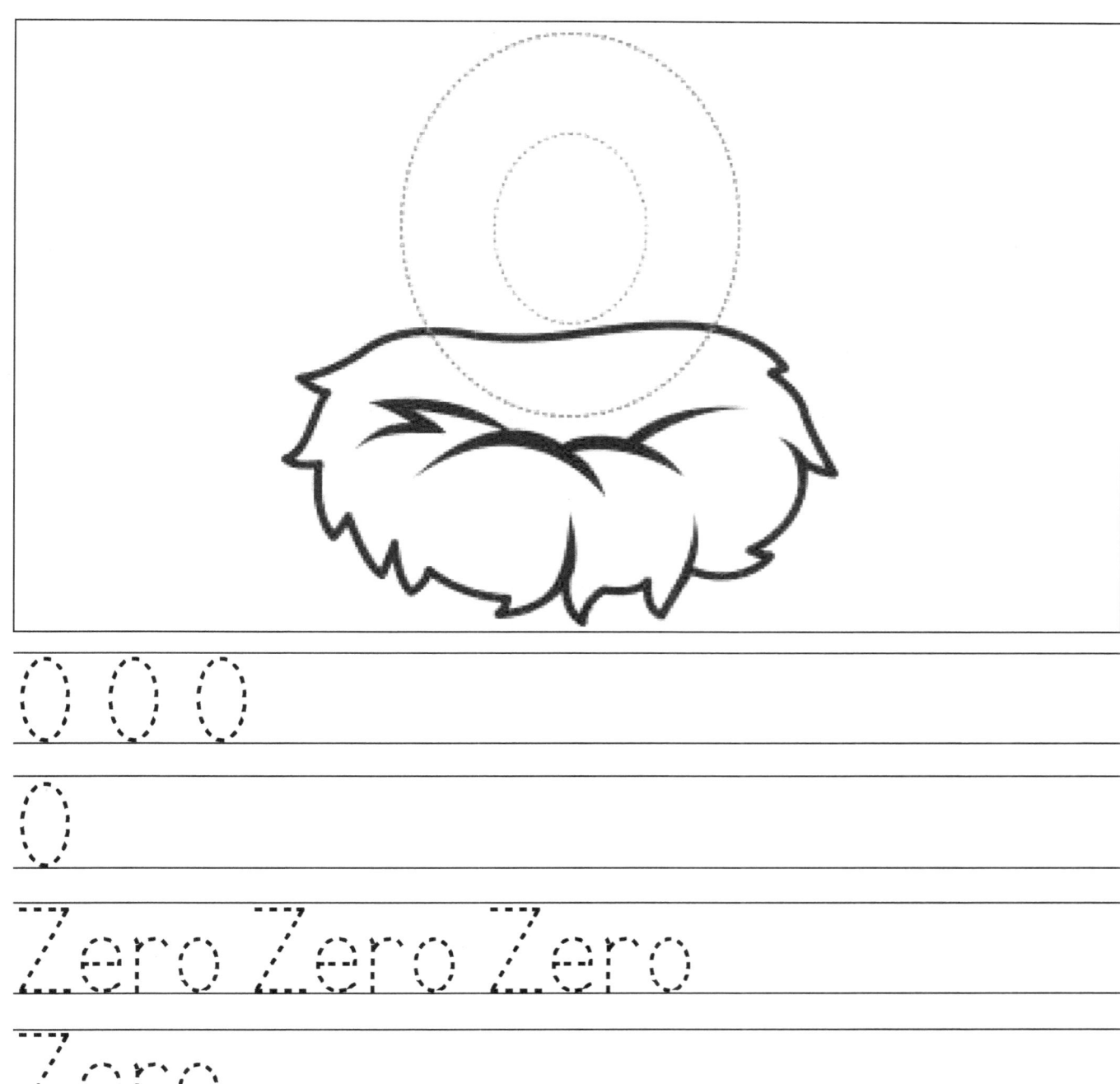

0
Zero
0
Zero
0
Zero
0
Zero
0
Zero
0

1 One

Trace the number and color picture.

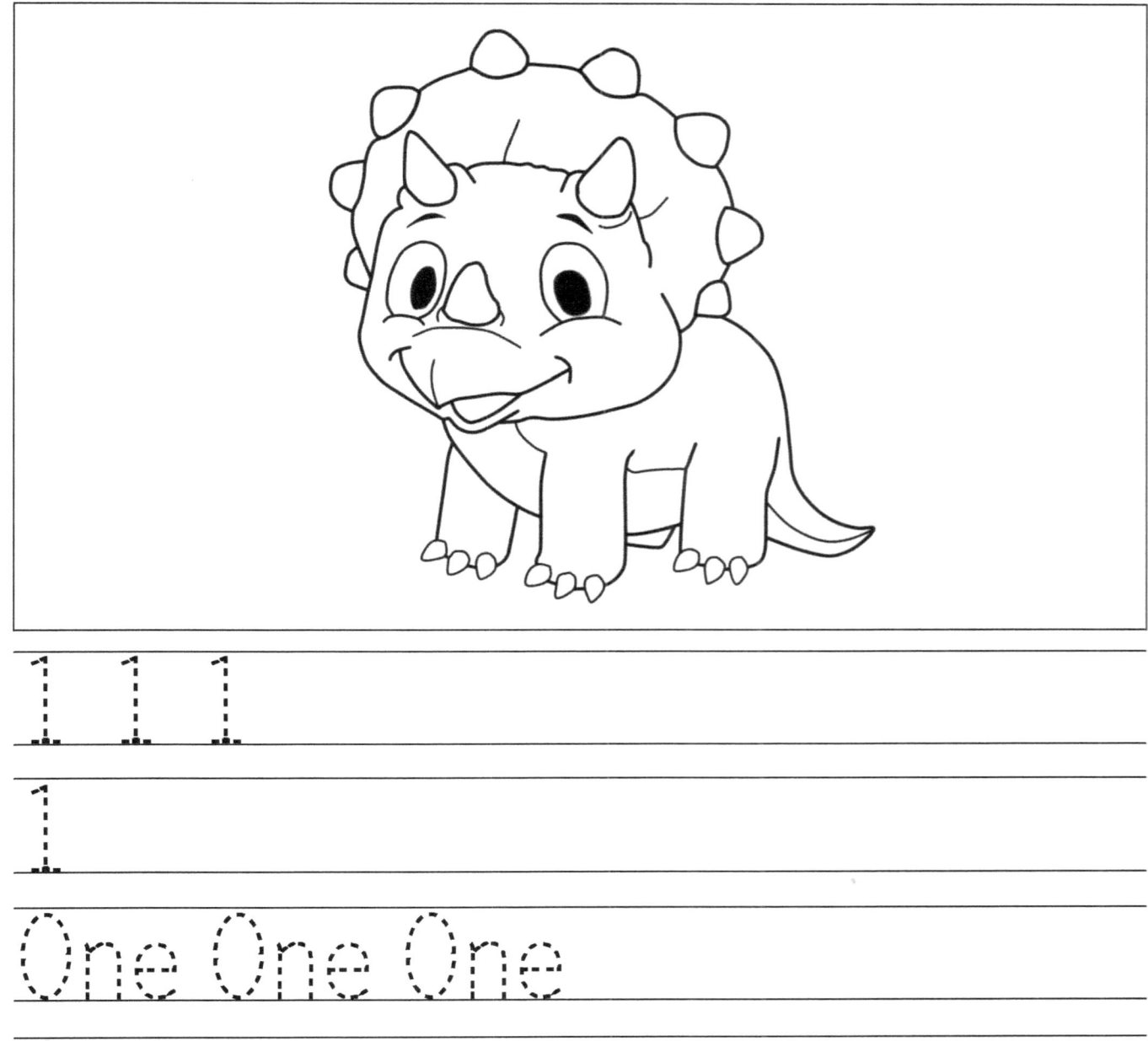

1 1 1

1

One One One

One

1
One
1
One
1
One
1
One
1
One
1

2 Two

Trace the number and color them.

2 2 2

2

Two Two Two

Two

2
Two
2
Two
2
Two
2
Two
2
Two
2

3 Three

Trace the number and color them.

3 3 3

3

Three Three Three

Three

3

Three

3

Three

3

Three

3

Three

3

Three

3

4 Four

Trace the number and color them.

4 4 4

4

Four Four Four

Four

4
Four
4
Four
4
Four
4
Four
4
Four
4

5 Five

Trace the number and color them.

5 5 5

5

Five Five Five

Five

5
Five
5
Five
5
Five
5
Five
5
Five
5

6 Six

Trace the number and color them.

6
Six
6
Six
6
Six
6
Six
6
Six
6

7 Seven

Trace the number and color them.

7 7 7

7

Seven Seven Seven

Seven

7

Seven

7

Seven

7

Seven

7

Seven

7

Seven

7

8 Eight

Trace the number and color them.

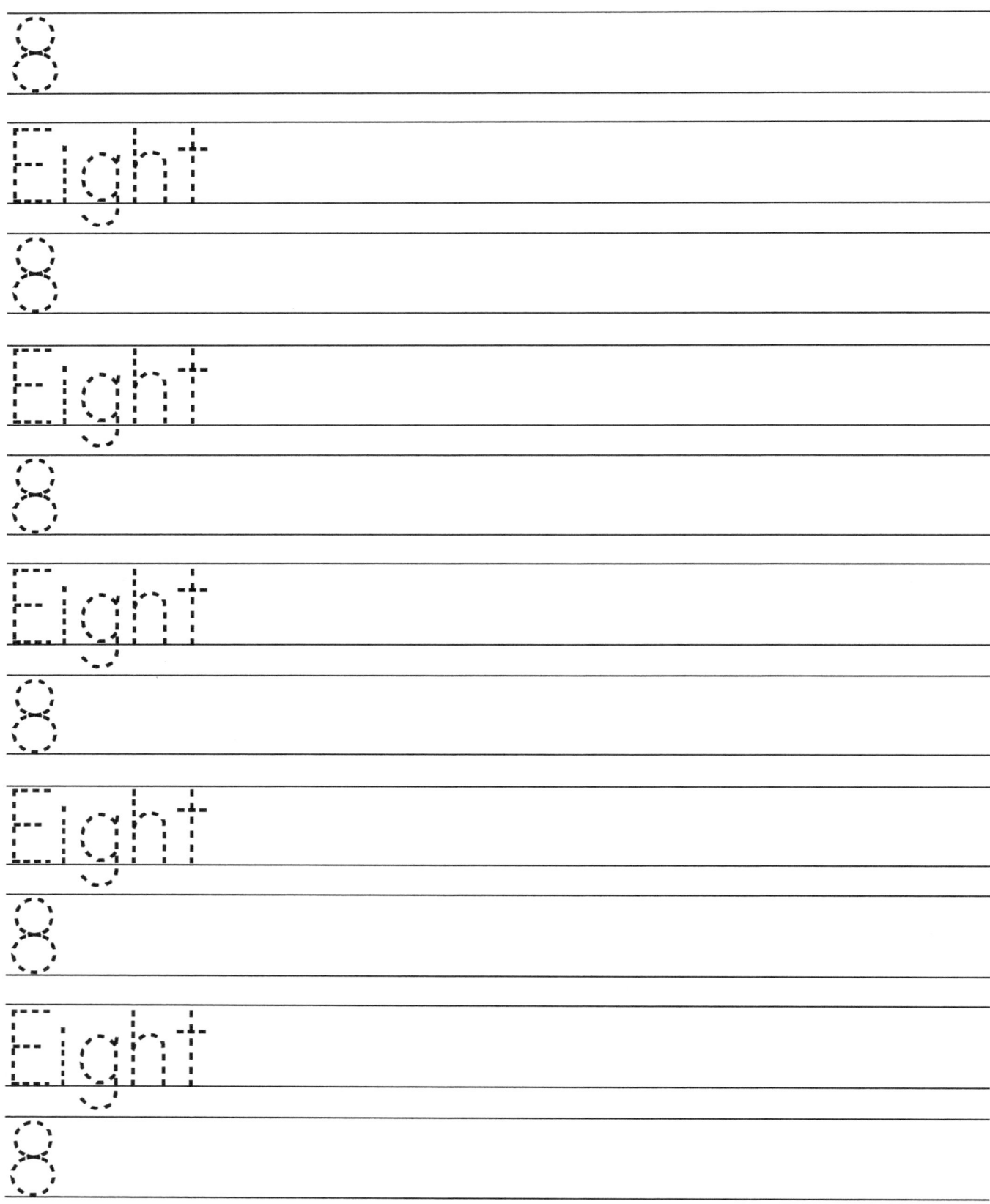

9 Nine

Trace the number and color them.

9 9 9

9

Nine Nine Nine

Nine

9

Nine

9

Nine

9

Nine

9

Nine

9

Nine

9

10 Ten

Trace the number and color them.

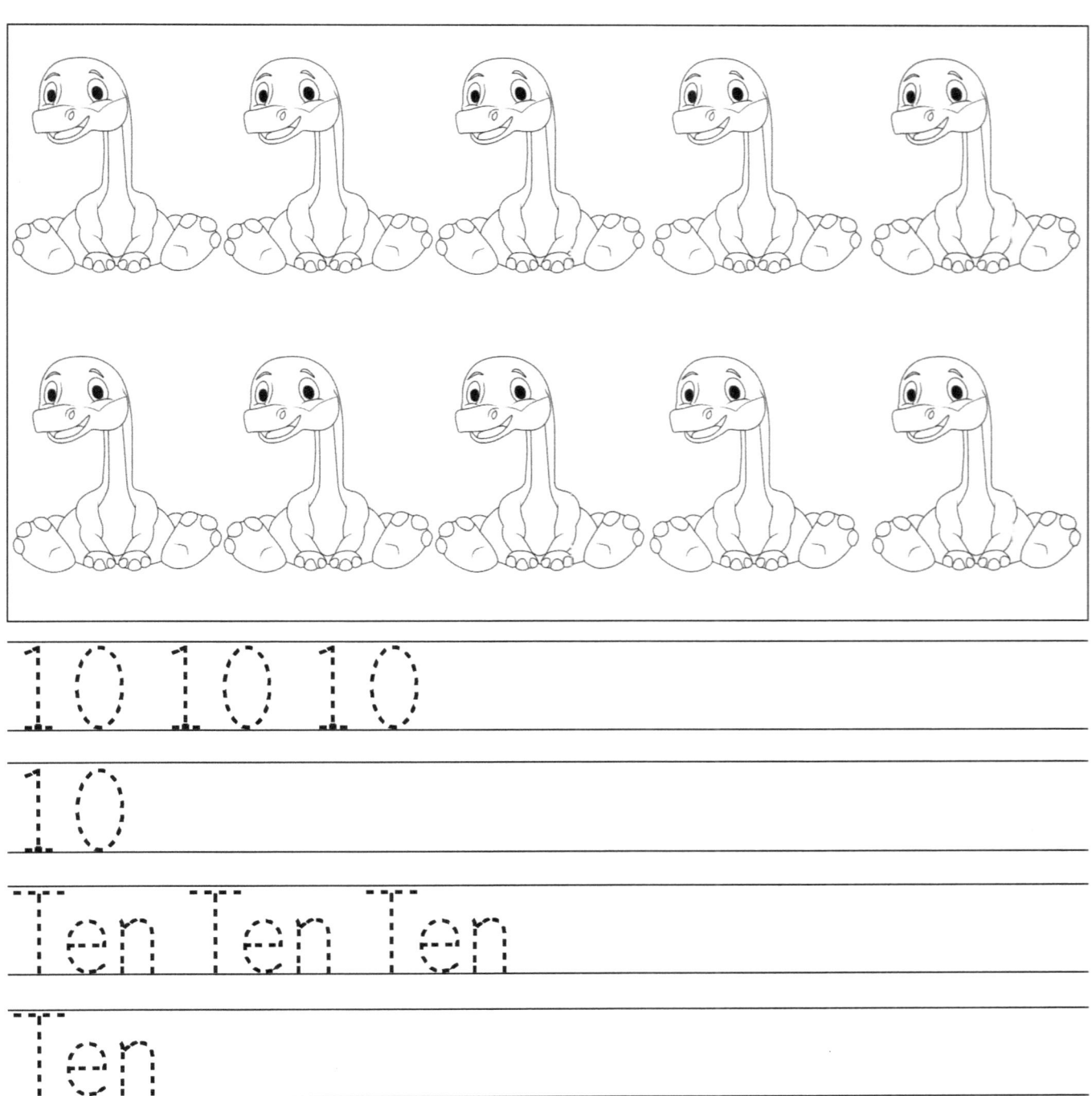

10 10 10

10

Ten Ten Ten

Ten

10
Ten
10
Ten
10
Ten
10
Ten
10
Ten
10

Circle and color the things you can find in which there are only **1** of each.

Circle and color the things you can find in which there are only **3** of each.

Circle and color the things you can find in which there are only **5** of each.

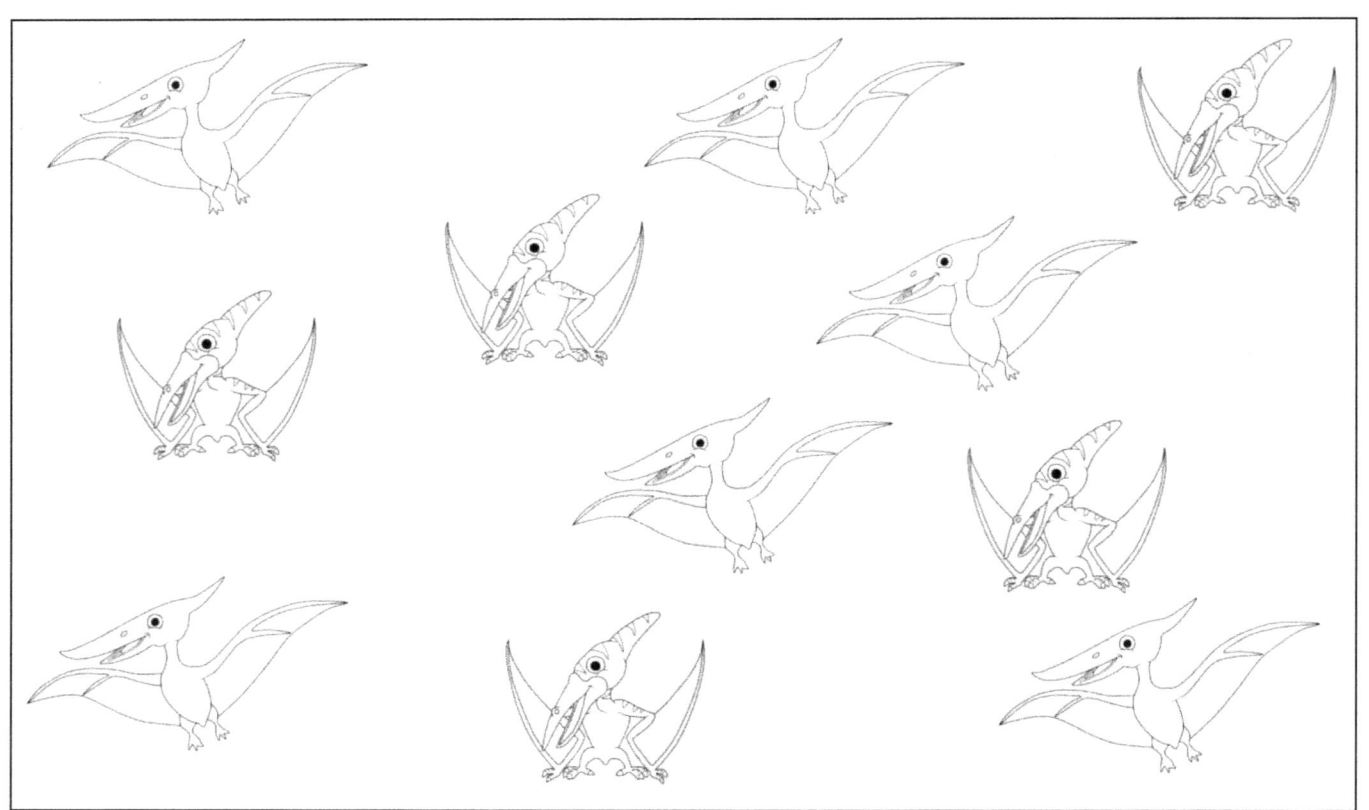

Circle and color the things you can find in which there are only **4** of each.

Let's Count!
Count each kind of dinosaurs and fill your answers in below.

How many ?_____

How many ?_____

Let's Count!
Count each kind of dinosaurs and fill your answers in below.

How many ? _____

How many ? _____

Let's Count!
Count each kind of dinosaurs and fill your answers in below.

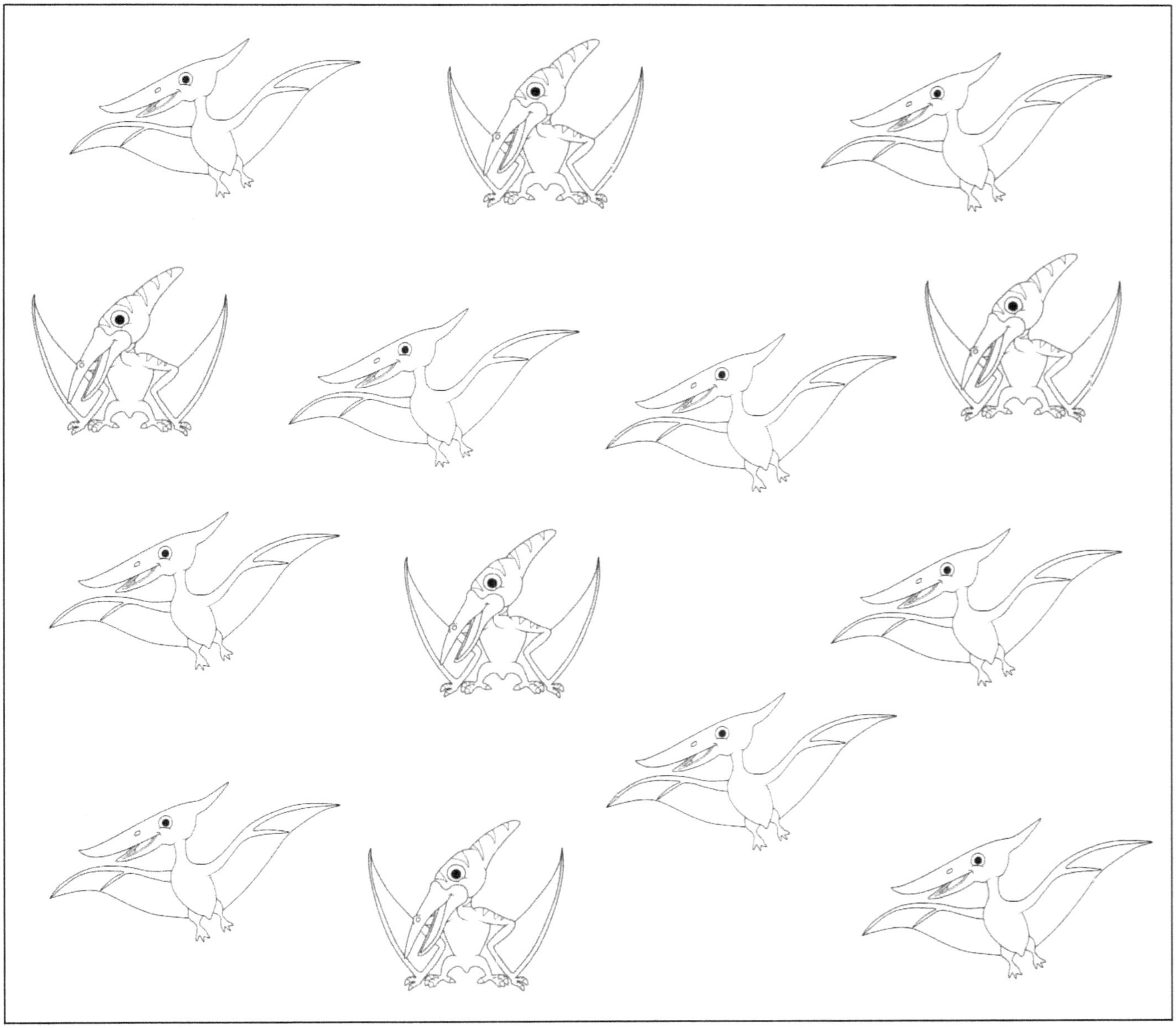

How many ?_____

How many ?_____

Let's Count!
Count each kind of dinosaurs and fill your answers in below.

How many ?_____

How many ?_____

Color the dinosaur eggs and Match the Number!

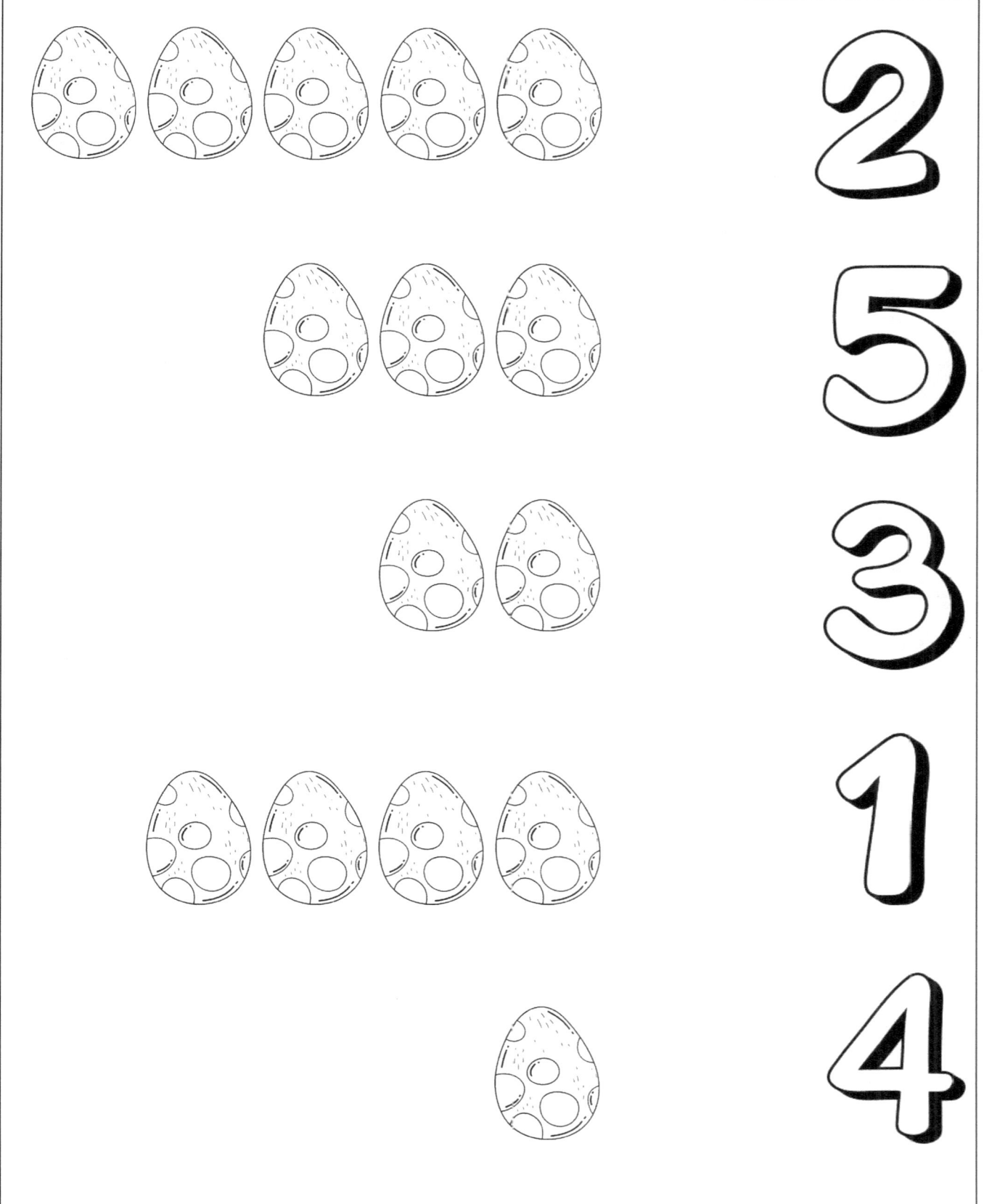

Color the dinosaur eggs and Match the Number!

Circle and color the dinosaur eggs set and matches the number!

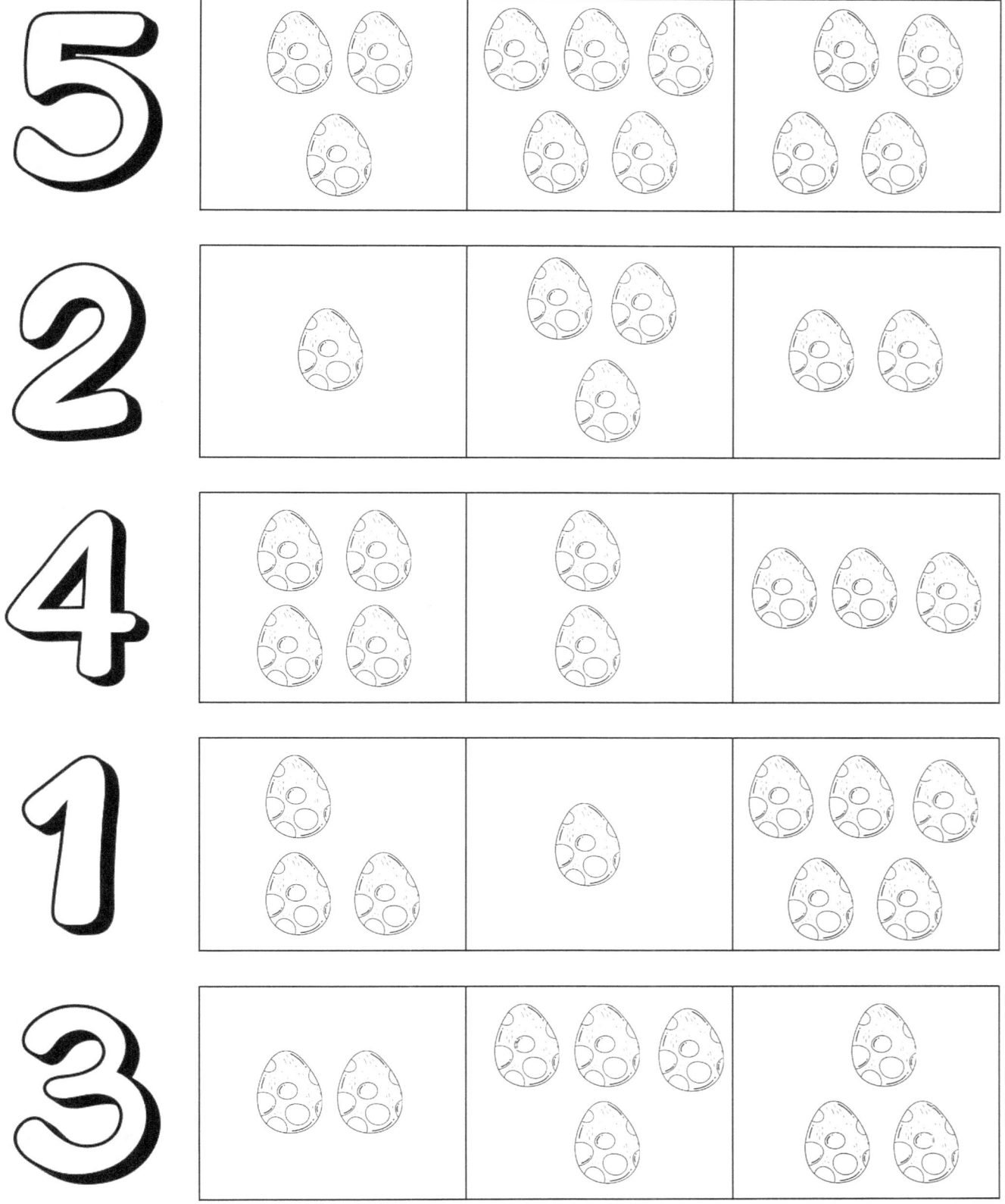

Circle the number that matches the set.

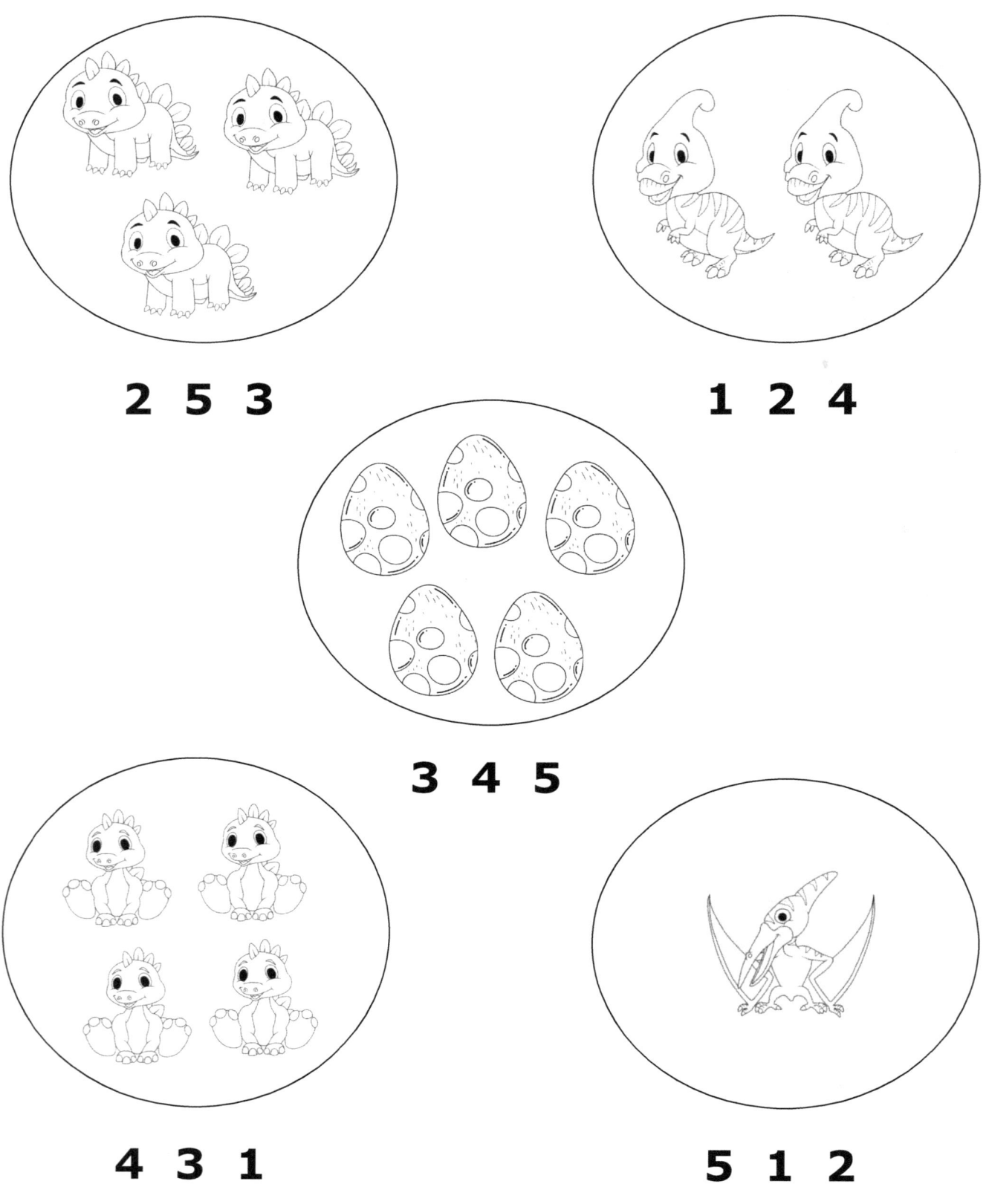

Circle and color the dinosaur eggs set and matches the number!

Circle the number that matches the set.

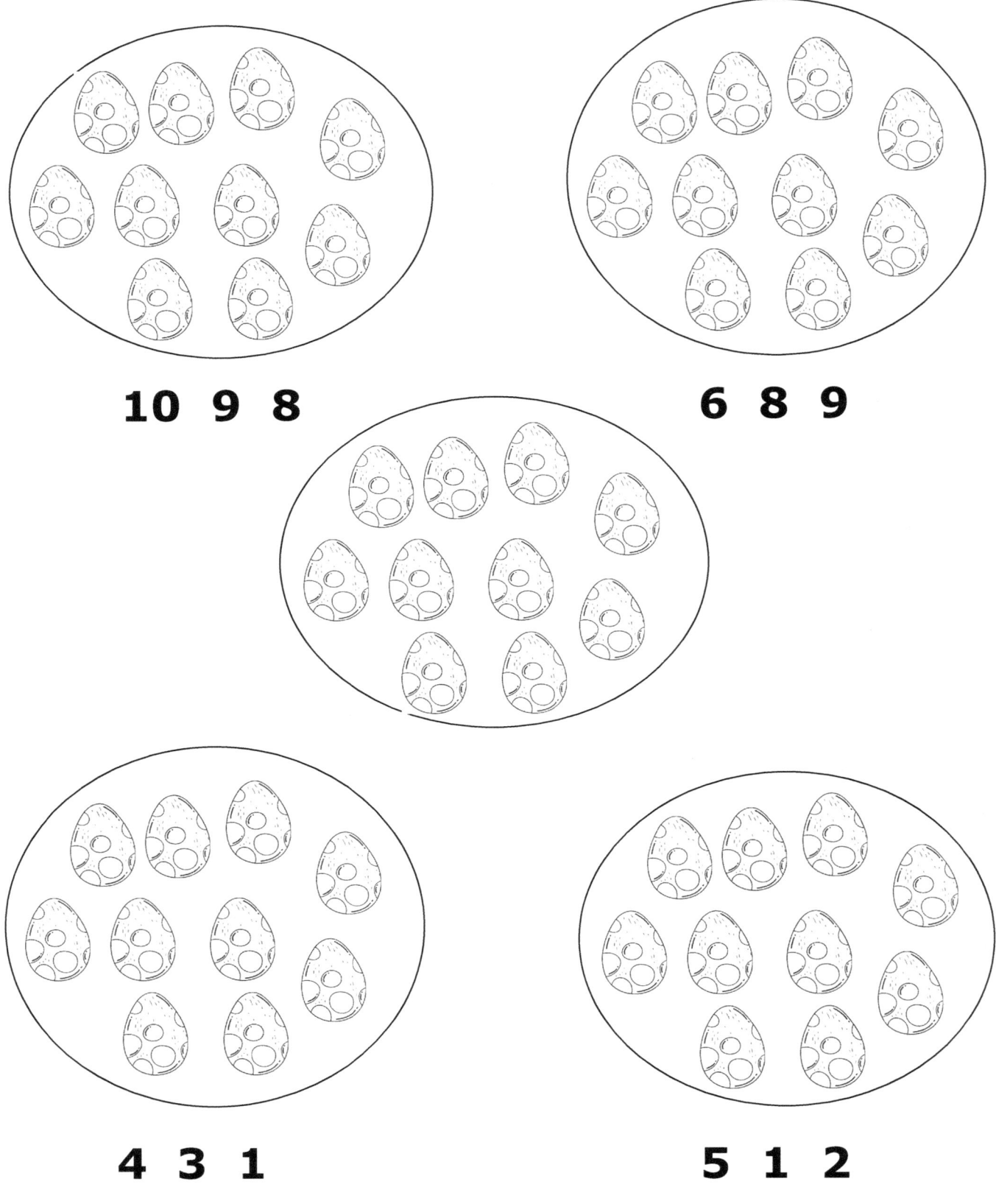

10 9 8   **6 8 9**

4 3 1   **5 1 2**

What a Difference
Look at the pictures below and draw a circle around the correct picture.

What a Difference

Look at the pictures below and draw a circle around the correct picture.

What a Difference
Color in the pictures. Make them all different!

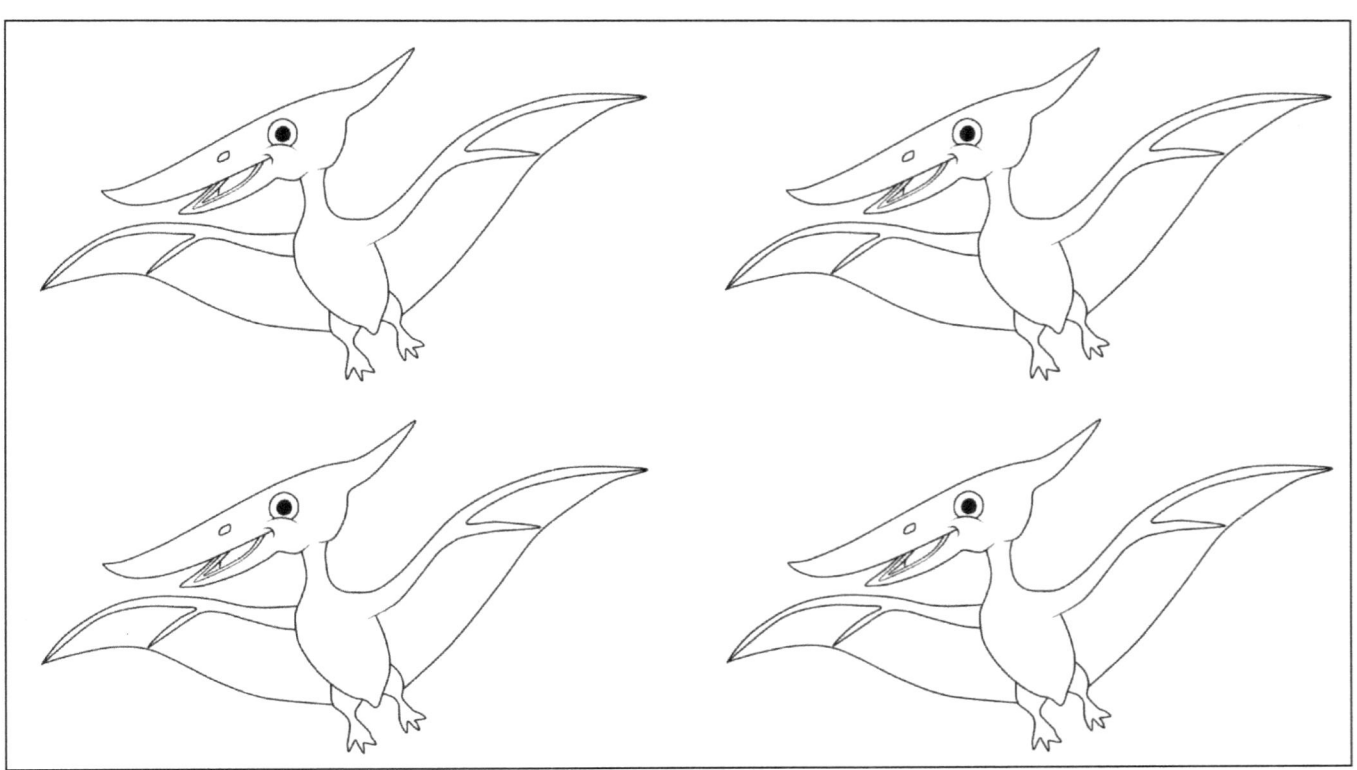

What a Difference
Color in the pictures. Make them all different!

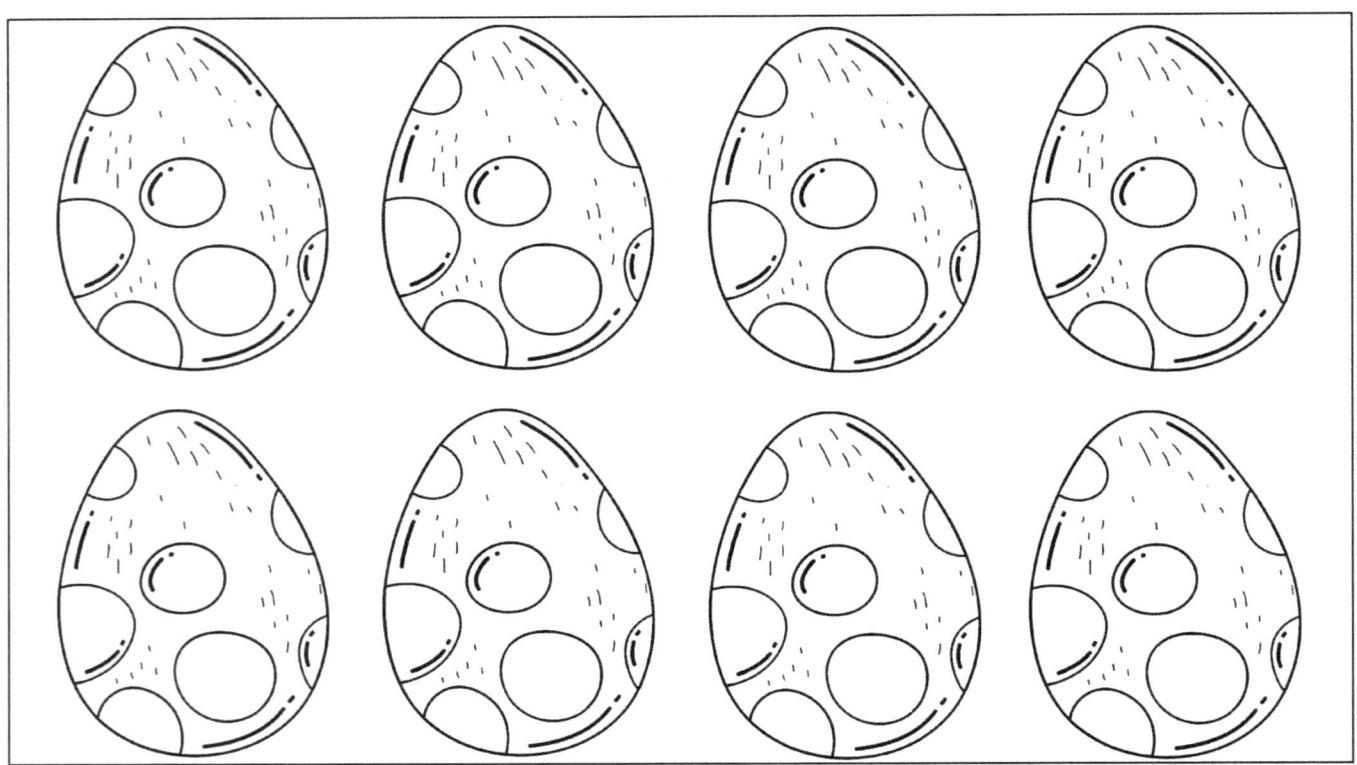

More or Less?

Look at the dinosaurs in each box and circle the group that has **more.**

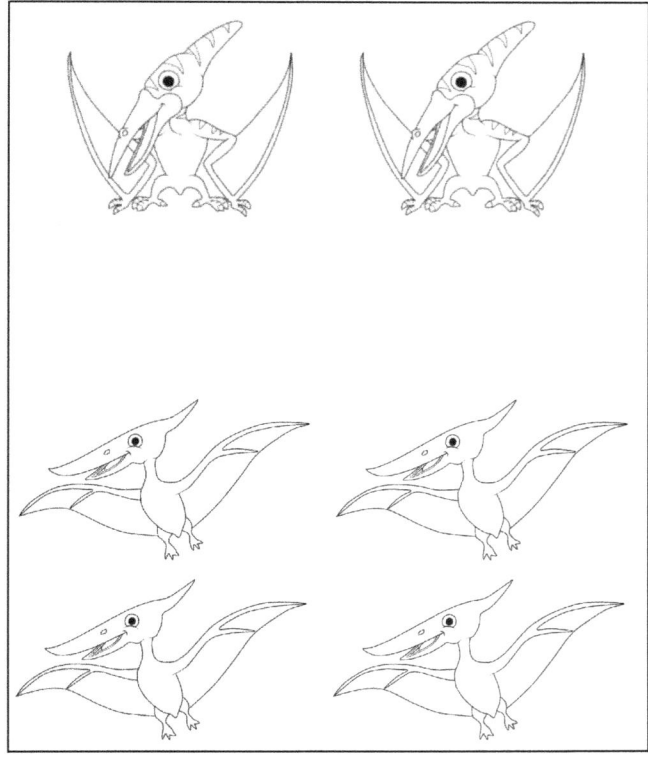

More or Less?

Look at the dinosaurs in each box and circle the group that has **more**.

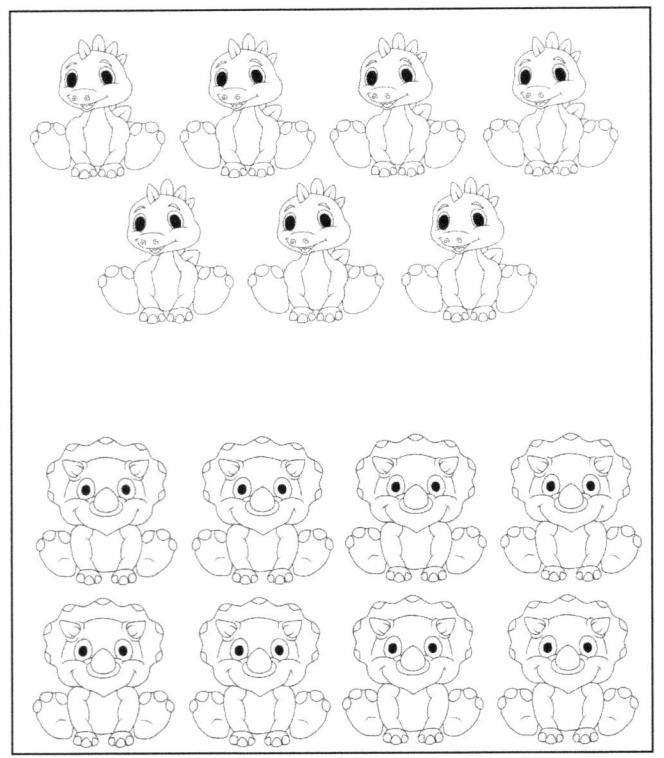

More or Less?

Look at the dinosaurs in each box and circle the group that has **less.**

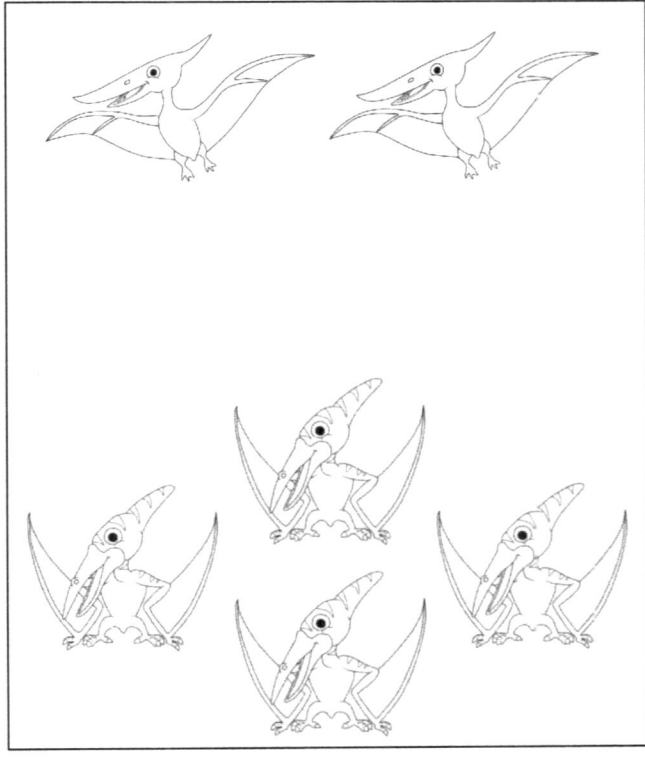

More or Less?

Look at the dinosaur in each box and circle the group that has **less.**

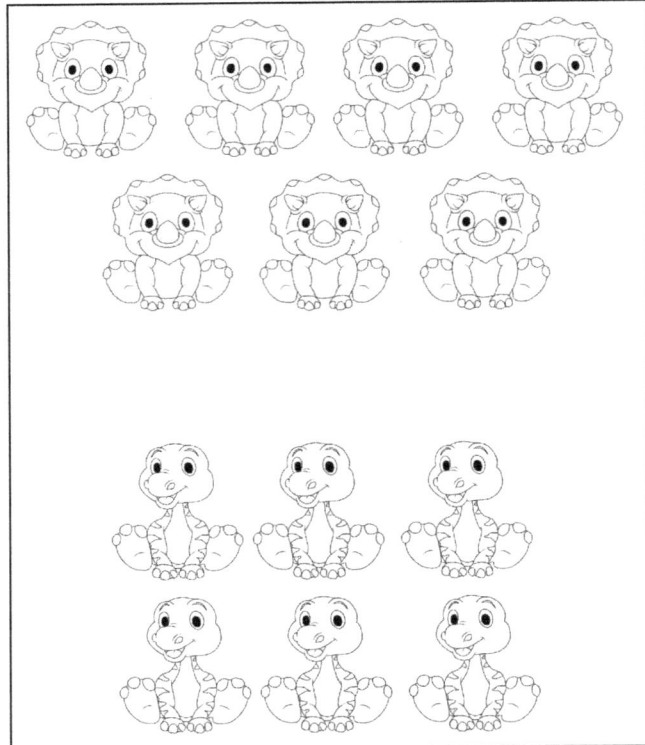

Big vs. Small

Look at the picture below and answer the question by circling the correct picture.

Big vs. Small

Look at the picture below and answer the question by circling the correct picture.

Which is **bigger?**

Which is **smaller?**

Which is **smaller?**

Which is **bigger?**

Big vs. Small

Look at the picture below and answer the question by drawing the correct picture.

Draw a **bigger**

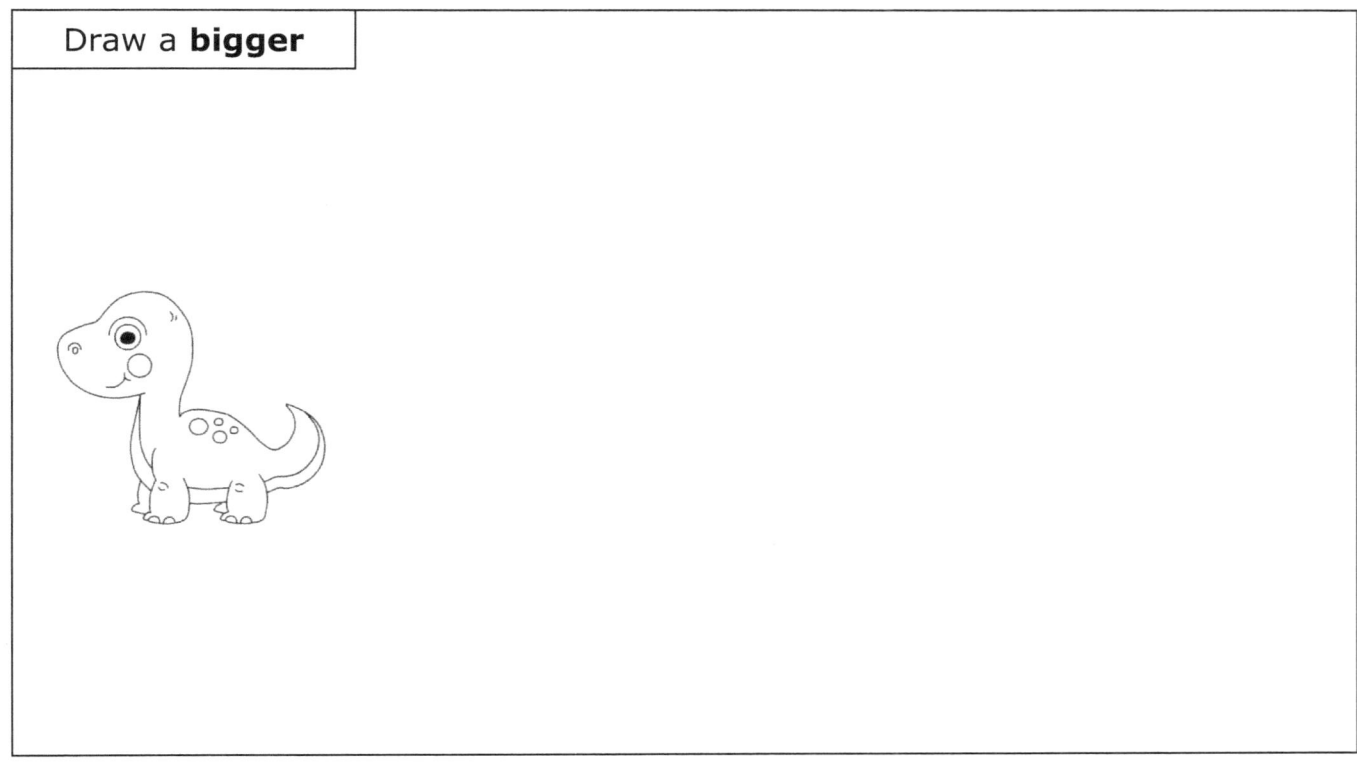

Draw a **smaller**

Big vs. Small

Look at the picture below and answer the question by drawing the correct picture.

Draw a **bigger**

Draw a **smaller**

Big vs. Small

Look at the picture below and answer the question by drawing the correct picture.

Draw a **bigger**

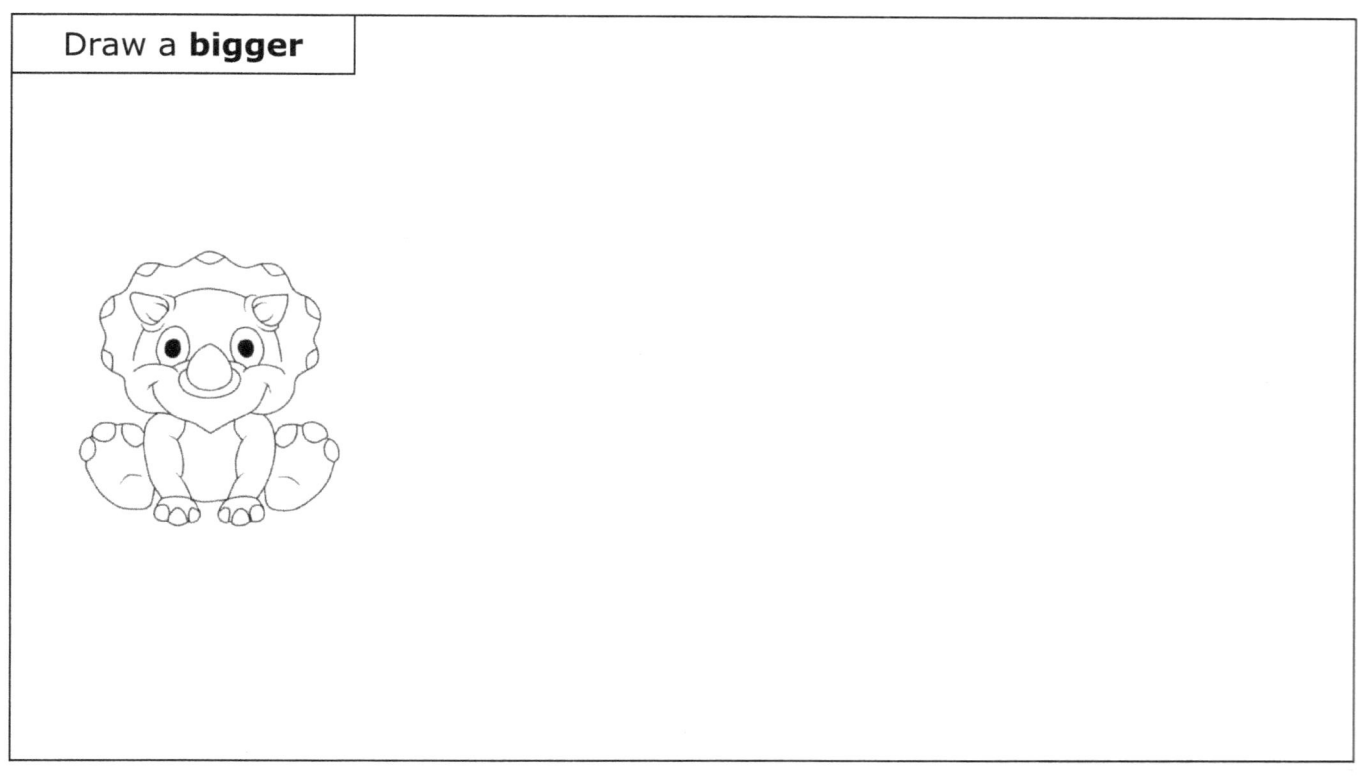

Draw a **smaller**

Big vs. Small

Look at the picture below and answer the question by drawing the correct picture.

Draw a **bigger**

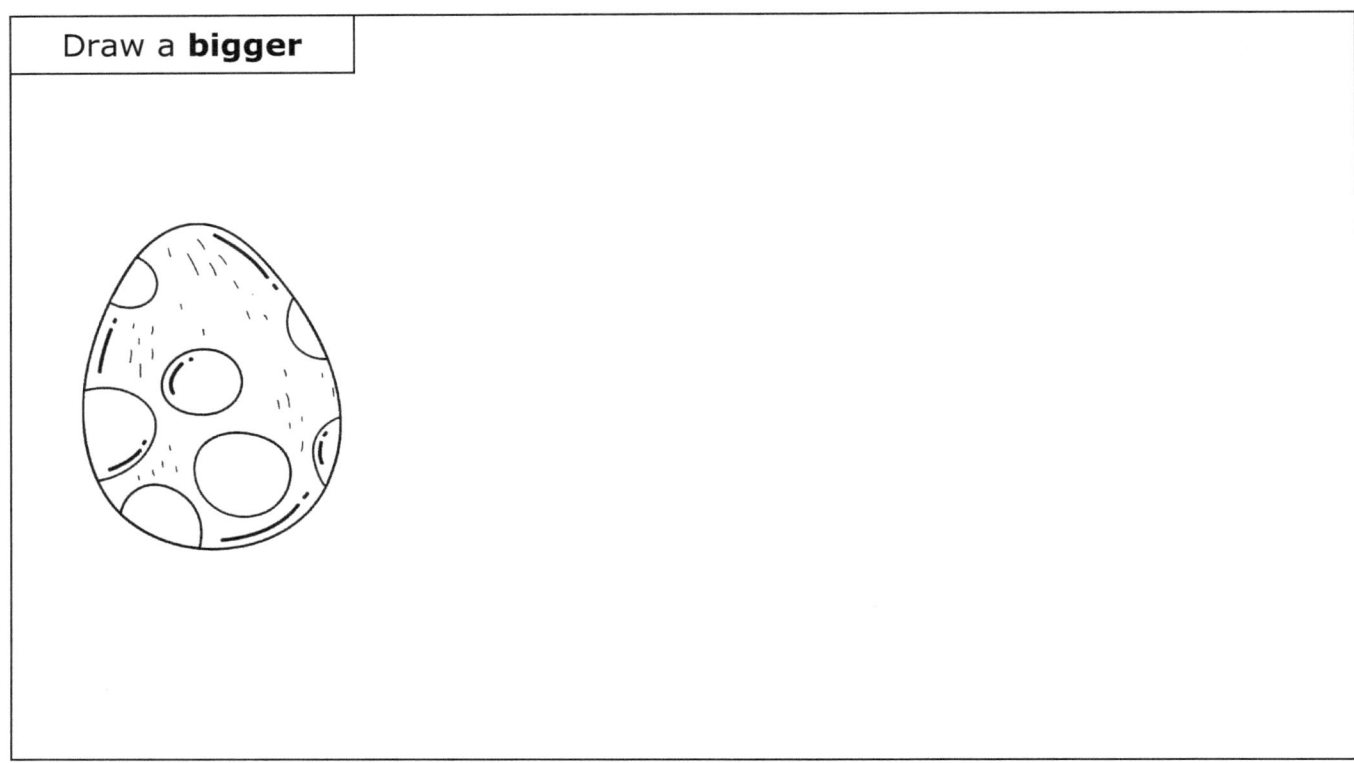

Draw a **smaller**

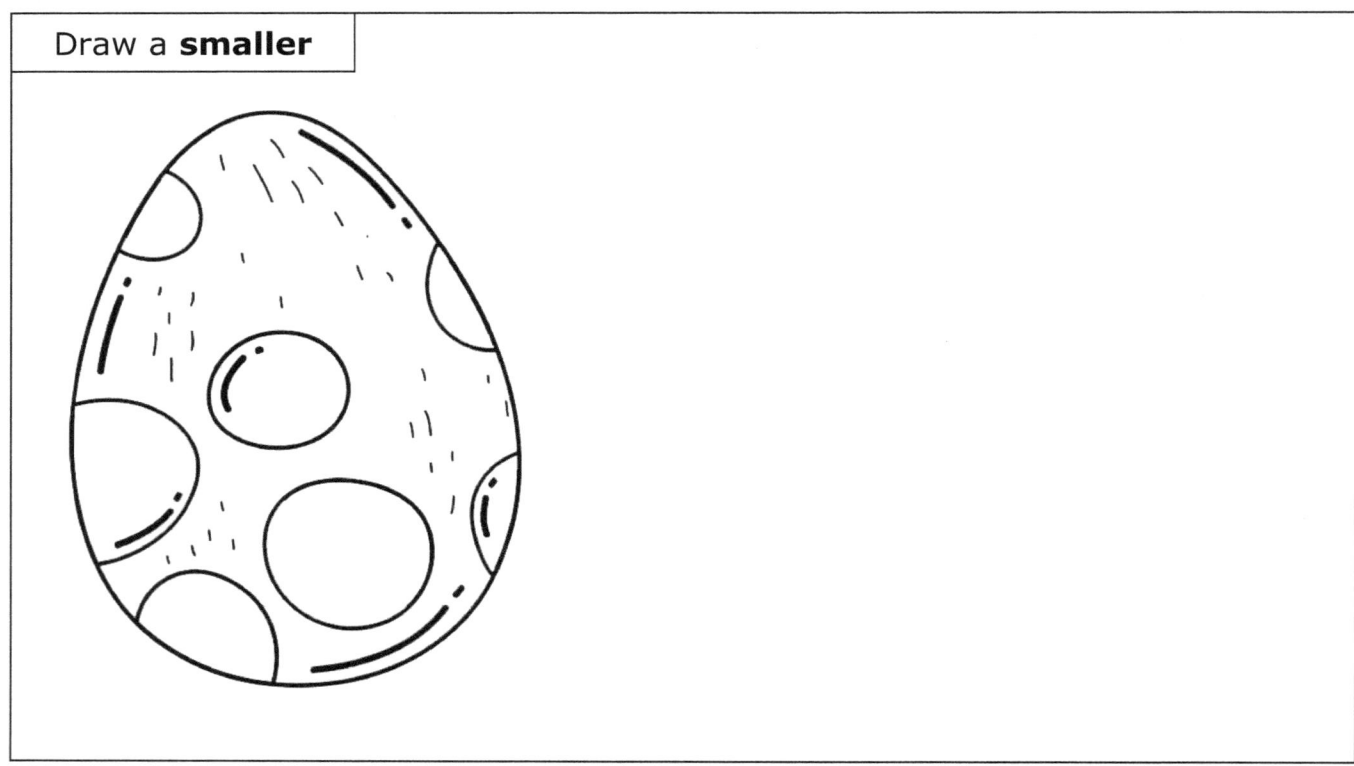

Compare sizes

Small   Medium   Large

Trace the shape.

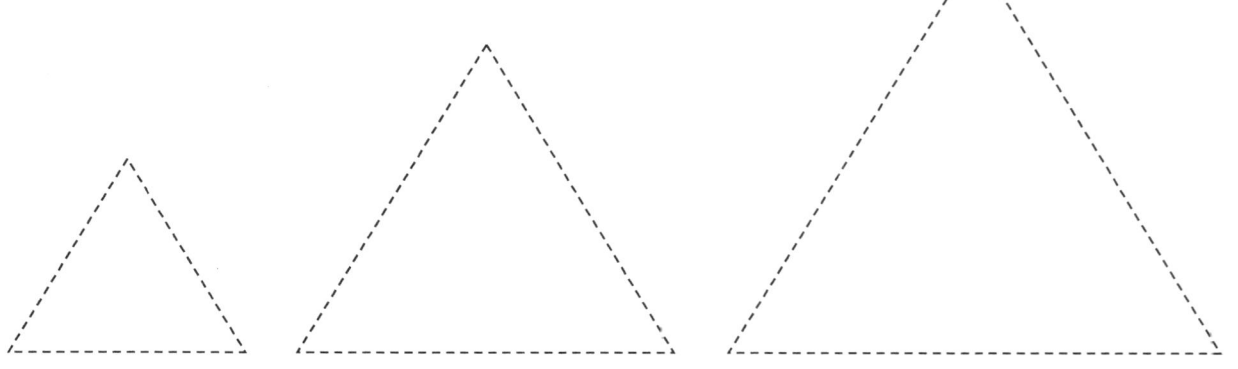

After tracing the shape, color the large in red, medium in yellow and small in green

Trace the shape.

After tracing the shape, color the large in red, medium in yellow and small in green

Compare sizes

Small Medium **Large**

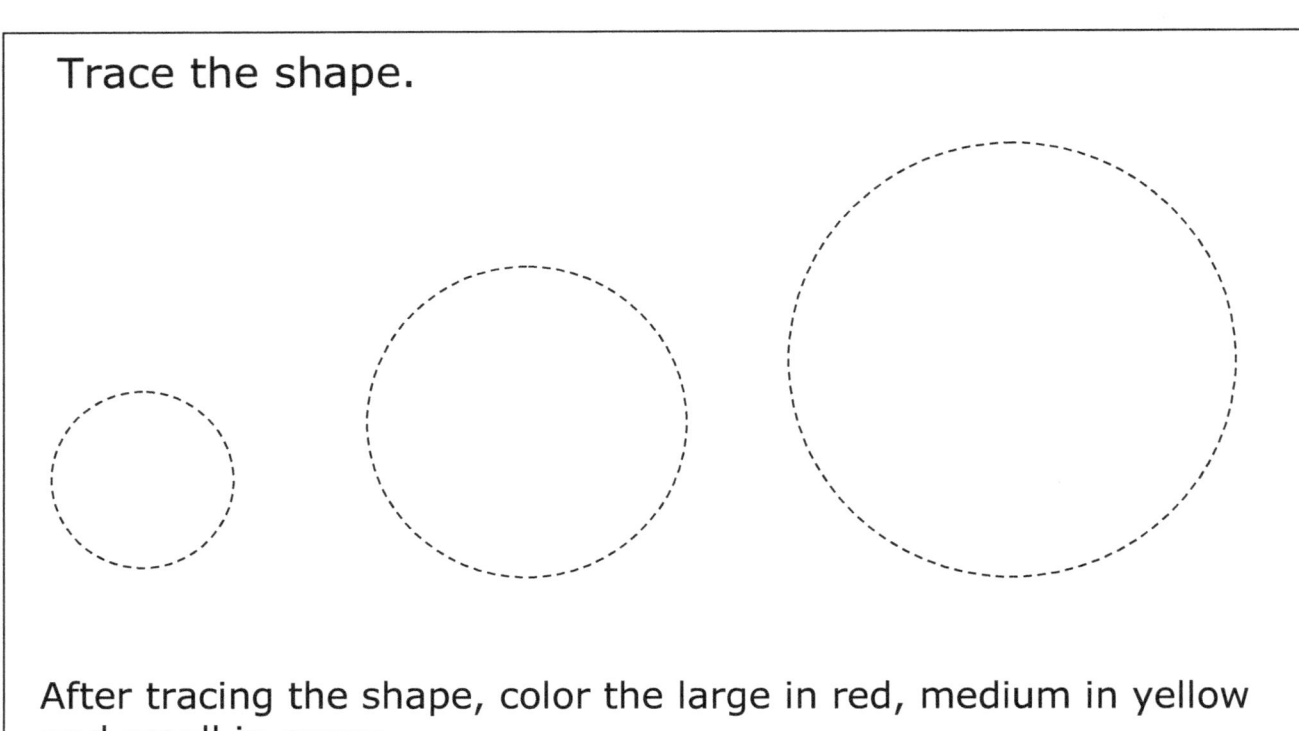

Trace the shape.

After tracing the shape, color the large in red, medium in yellow and small in green

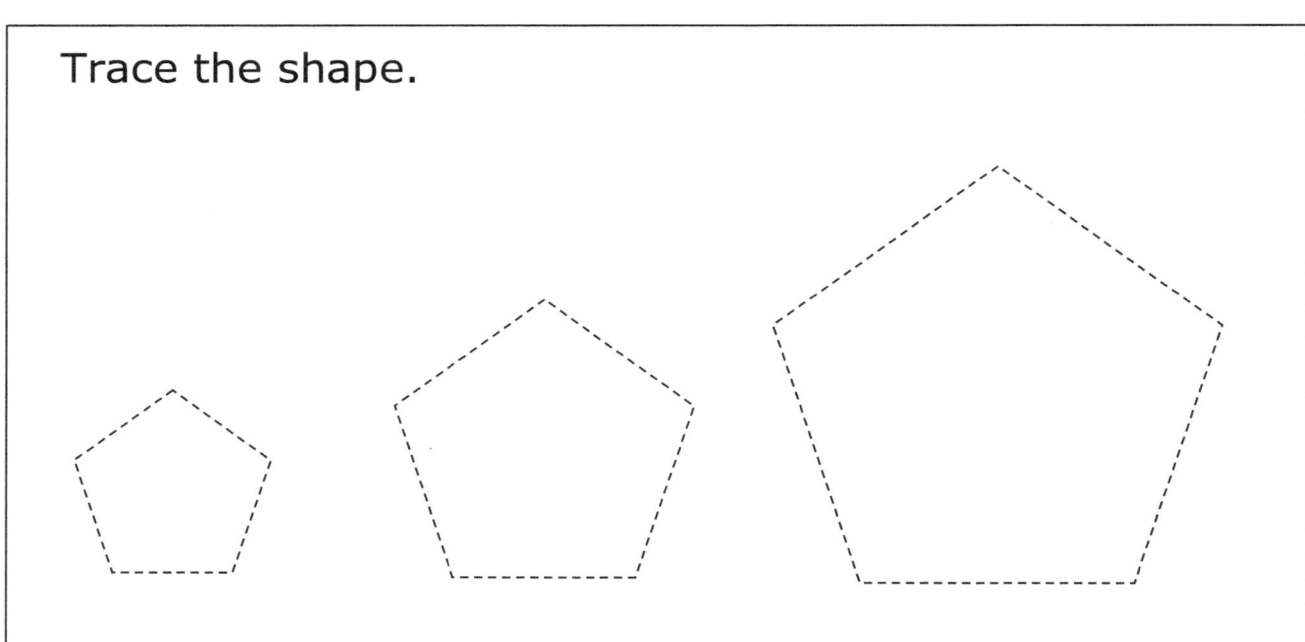

Trace the shape.

After tracing the shape, color the large in red, medium in yellow and small in green

Compare sizes

Draw the missing shape and color them.

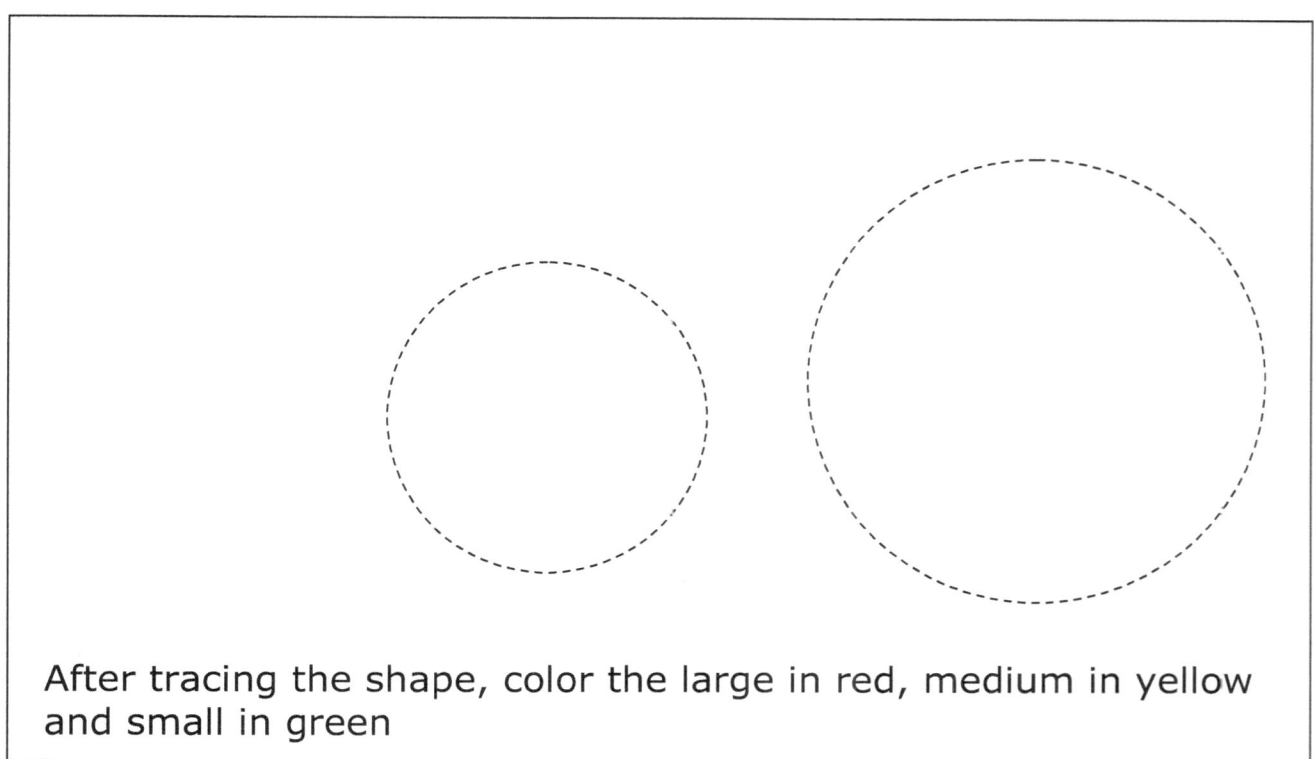

After tracing the shape, color the large in red, medium in yellow and small in green

Trace the shape.

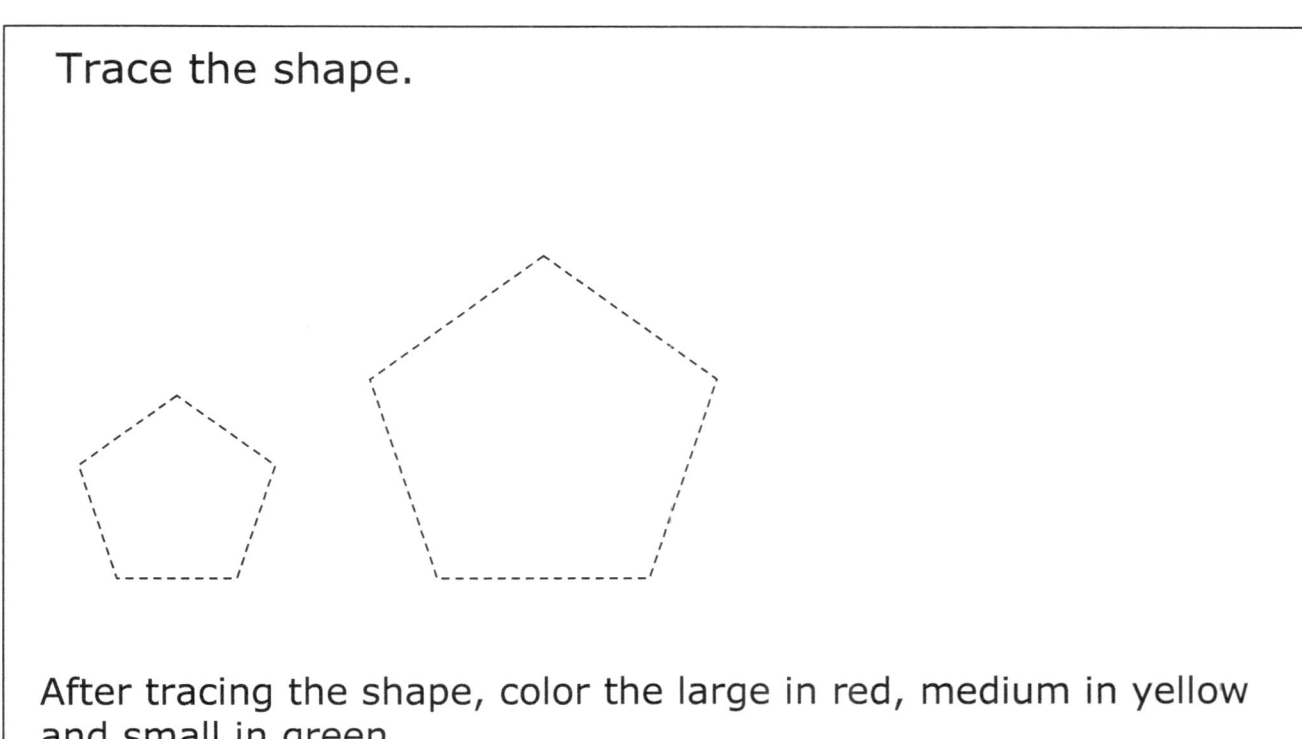

After tracing the shape, color the large in red, medium in yellow and small in green

Compare sizes

Draw the missing shape and color them.

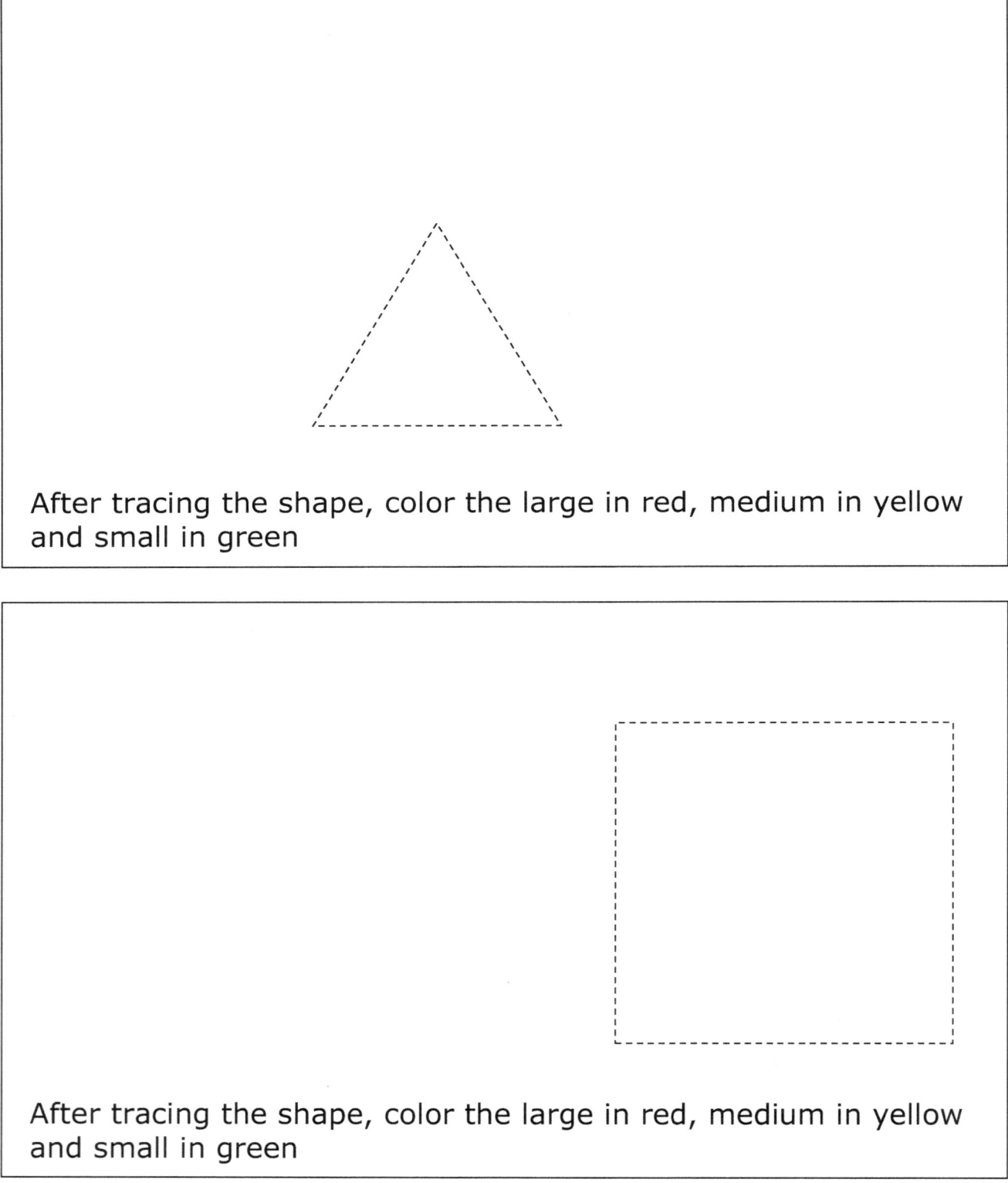

After tracing the shape, color the large in red, medium in yellow and small in green

After tracing the shape, color the large in red, medium in yellow and small in green

Circle the picture that comes next!

Circle the picture that comes next!

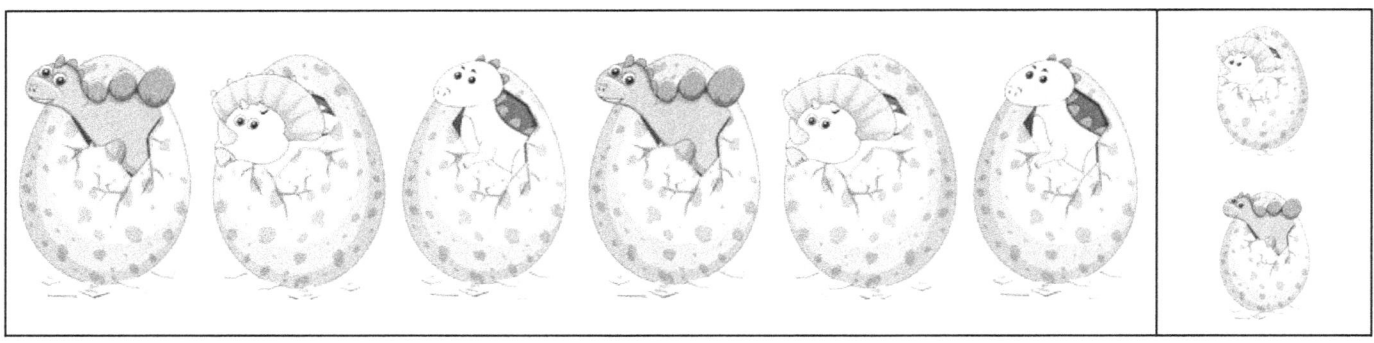

Number Fun

Counting up from 1, which number comes next?

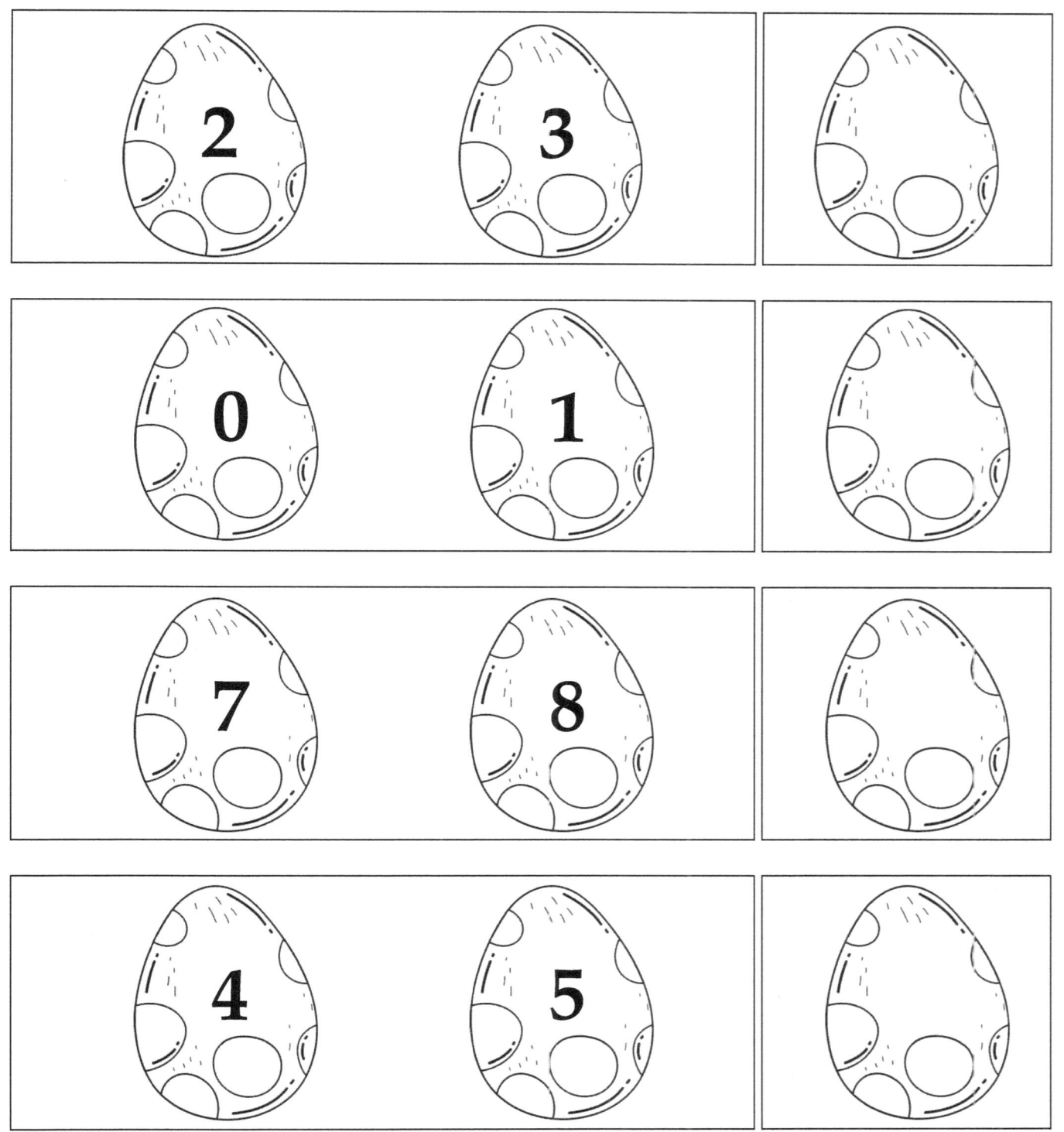

Number Fun

Counting up from 1, which number comes next?

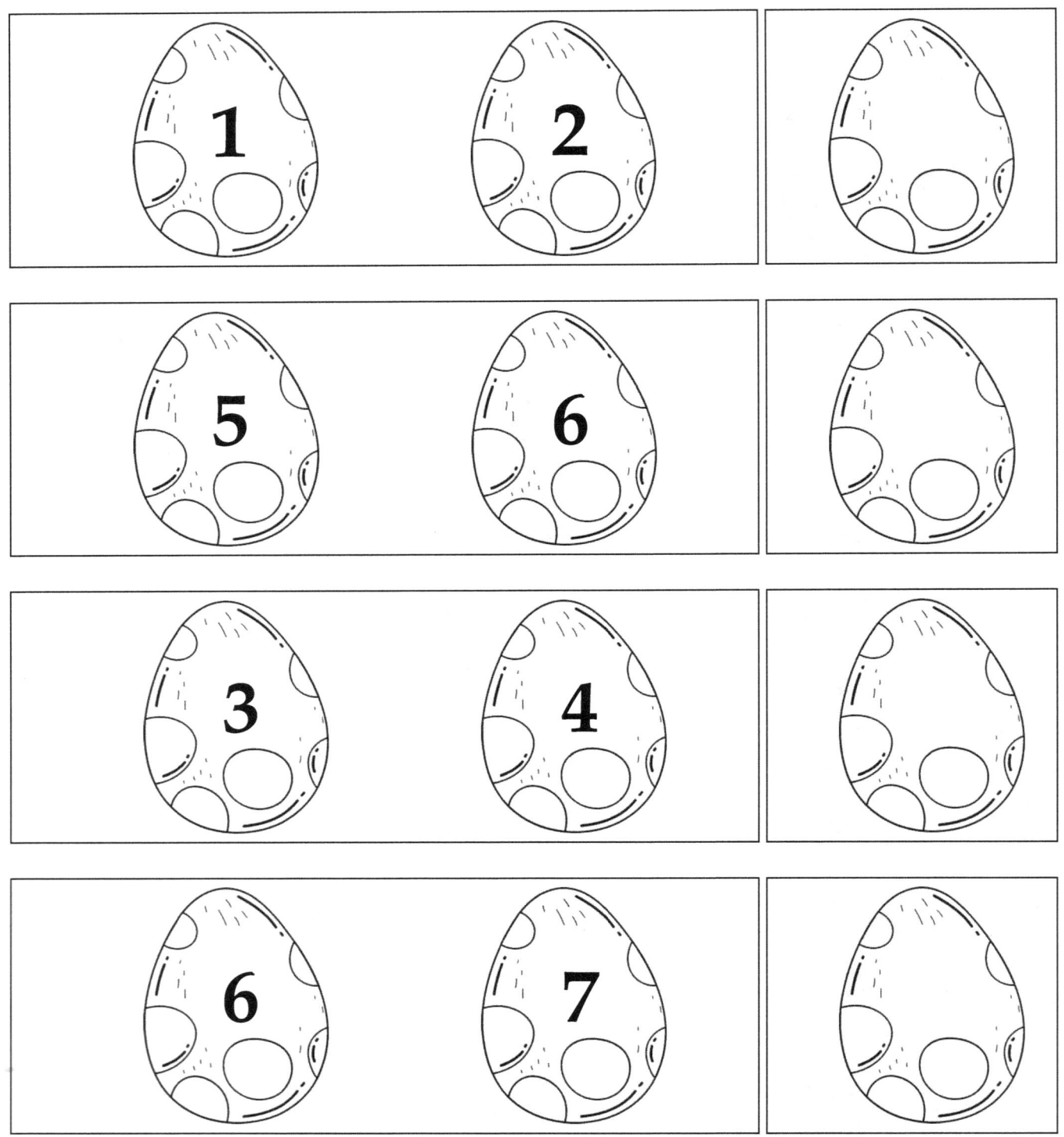

Number Fun

Counting forward from **4**

Counting forward from **2**

Counting forward from **1**

Counting forward from **7**

Number Fun

Counting forward from **3**

 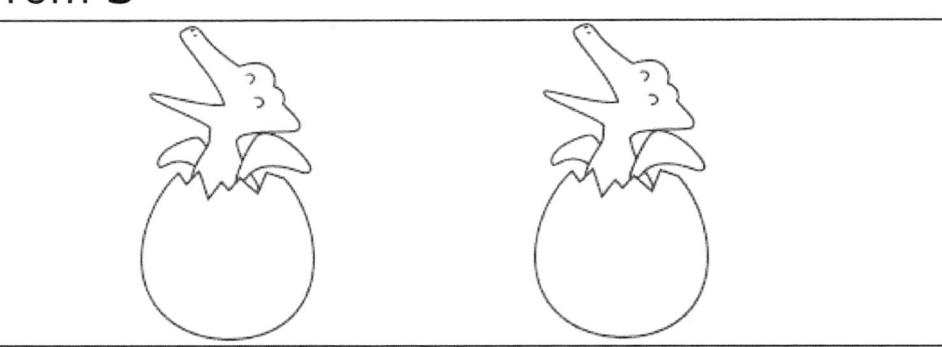

Counting forward from **6**

 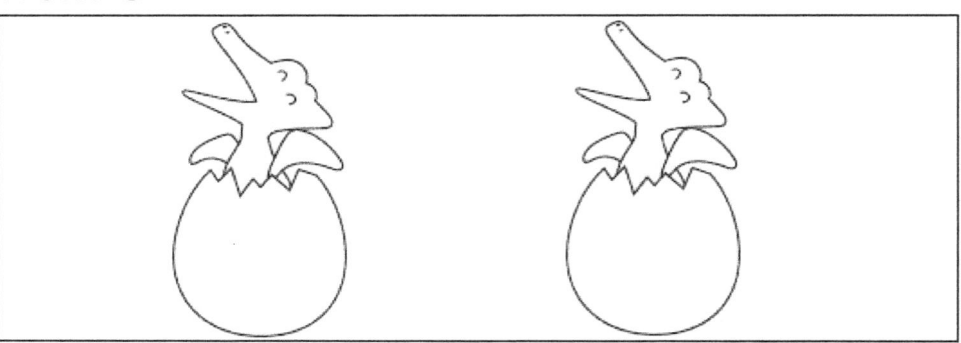

Counting forward from **0**

 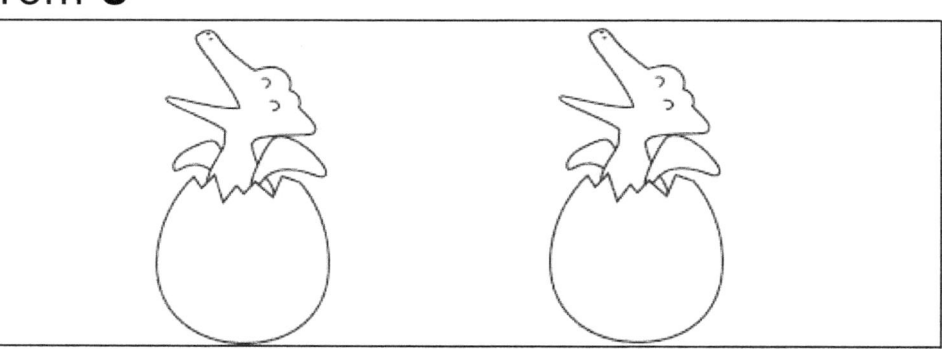

Counting forward from **7**

Number Fun

Find number in the animals and compare, then color the one containing the larger number.

Number Fun

Find number in the animals and compare, then color the one containing the larger number.

DATE: _____

TIME: _____

Thank you!

Thank you for buying "Dinosaur Preschool Basics Workbook" we would be more than happy to consider how to apply your suggestion to the next edition. Without you voice, we can't exist.

Please, support us and leave a review!
We welcome your positive feedback and hope that others will benefit from your experience.

CPSIA information can be obtained
at www.ICGtesting.com
Printed in the USA
BVHW012128180420
577900BV00015B/1212